I

The Skullfuck Collection

Jeremy Void

To Deane

Other books by Jeremy Void

Derelict America
(short stories and essays)

Nefarious Endeavors
(short stories and some poetry)

Smash a Lightbulb:
Poetry for Lowlifes
(poetry, prose, creative essays, and more)

Erase Your Face:
The SkullFuck Collection
(visual poetry)

Just a Kid
(experimental prose and poetry)

Sex Drugs & Violence:
Incomplete Stories for the Incomplete Human
(incomplete stories)

An Art Form:
The Crass Poetry Collection
(poetry)

My Story:
The Short Version
(my own personal drunkalogue)

I
NEED
HELP

The SkullFuck Collection

Jeremy Void

I Need Help: The SkullFuck Collection

Copyright © 2015 by Jeremy Void

ISBN Number:
978-0-578-16528-8

ChaosWriting Press

IT'S A MINDFUCK
www.chaoswriting.net

To

You

Jeremy Void at 18
his ID picture

Author's Note:

This is my eighth book. It is a continuation of the SkullFuck Collection, first seen in my book *Erase Your Face.*

In the making of *Erase Your Face,* I did not have Photoshop, so I designed every piece on Microsoft Word. It wasn't until much later when I obtained Photoshop on my computer.

So I Need Help is a lot more interactive; it's a lot more expansive. In so many ways. I'm proud of every new book when it comes out—as my best book is always the last one I did, in my own opinion—but this one is beyond anything I've ever done, in more ways than one.

It's edgy, it's fun, it's weird, and it's provocative. It's all things and more.

It is my hope that in reading this book you don't just whizz through it, but instead read and observe the piece in question, really sit down with it, digest it, before going on to the next one.

That said, I hope you enjoy this book. I know I sure have.

Introduction

I don't love a whole lot. I might have loved you way back when but that has passed and now I'm here, today is not yesterday, nor is it tomorrow. Today is today, and yesterday I soared in the clouds with vicious bats. Tomorrow I might climb a mountain, but today this muse is shoutin for me to create something worth viewing—something higher than might but smaller than that which bites. Words are the love of my life, the thing that keeps me going when all is down and the bets are rattling at me telling me to quit.

I fall asleep as streams of words pour from my mind, I walk through a matrix of words as they buzz past my sight. I listen to the words; they speak to me, they glow and fluctuate in the night. They stand above everything and when I die, these words will whisk me up to heaven

so I can say goodbye.

"Our concrete poems are Shit/ each poem a tiny spat of diarrrrrhea growing into infinite globules of cement excrement/ our concrete poems are beyond concrete poems/ Where DaDaism failed, preaching Anti-Art but creating ant & the NaDaists failed by creating art of nothing-ness when they proclaimed NOTHING—the cleveland cement fuckers will succeed in giving the Public Shit."

— d. a . levy

it ⇒

begins

here.................
↑ **NOW**

Enter at your

own risk

1

Not for the squeamish
the sensitive
the overly dramatic
or those with their heads too
far up their asses

I pledge defiance to the Government of the United States of America and the injustice for which it stands; one nation above God, divisible and quite corruptible, with liberty and justice for some.

It's not all angry
not entirely hateful
nor dark
It has it's positive side too
Like a yin-yang
it's got the best of both worlds

the BEST of both worlds

4

F F   F F

U U   U U

F F F F C C

U U C C U U

C C K K C C K K

K K A A K K A A

A A R R A A R R

R R T T R R T T

T T   T T

5

You Made Me

and ⟶

you

wonder

why I hate

if you're offended by this book

good

because I'm offended by the way I had to grow up

so who's really been slighted

WORD ATTACK

WORD ATTACK

fight back

7

BREAKDOWN

BREAKDOWN

BREAKDOWN

BREAKDOWN

BREAKDOWN

BREAKDOWN

BREAKDOWN

Kids from all over meet here…

**kids swirl and swirl
they flail and they twirl
elbows and fists
kicks and jabs**

it's demolition dancing

The drummer drums
The guitarest strums
The bassist plucks
The singer lurches onstage

9

Another Xperimental Poem for Your Viewing Pleasure

And the poem begins

itisfastpaced, but s o m e t i m e s slows down

thenpicksupspeedand p
l
u
m
m
e
t
s to the ground
it can be   it can be
manic   t   depressing
h
It could start a riot   e
It could install order
w
r
i
t
e j
r' o
s b is to provoke
bring the 5 senses <<< meaning <<< emotions
to life——that is soundsmelltouchtaste and
H E A R I N G !!!
Dammit—I meant sight ^^^^^^^^^

10

FUCK THE SOCIAL CONTRACT
I signed nothing

X	fuck you

CAN'T CLASSIFY
IT DON'T WANT YOUR
LABELS DON'T MEAN
NOTHING IS ALL WE KNOW
ABOUT [IT] [IT] [IT] IS ART

i'm bored
i'm bored
i'm bored
i'm bored
i'm bored
i'm bored
i'm bored

i am bored
i am bored

Nothing to do // Nothing to do
Nothing to do // Nothing to do

13

How many Punks does it take
to screw in a lightbulb?

1 to screw it in.
1 to hold the ladder.
1 to talk about how punk this is.
and 1 to call everyone a poser and
leave.

Love that joke cuz of how
true it is. **So true.**

14

Alcoholic
Ambivalence

a CUNT RAWKer

a more lucid more destructive form of Punk.

Punk these days has become rather lame.
It's turned into a mob of pretty boys and wannabes.

I'm no Punk—I listen to Punk rock
but, really, I'm just a cunt
a cunt rawker.

It's raw, what you see is what you'll get.

17

The walls are
closing in on me

HELP
ME
!   !
.   .

The sky is
The sky is
falling on me
falling on me
falling on me

at least I'm doing
s o m e t h i n g
with my life!
what the hell
have you done?

Ignorant minds think alike

and that is why ...

the **WORLD**

as we know it

is going

straight to

HELL

Death Defying Stunts

1. Drove into a tree head-on and at full speed
2. Climbed out of a pickup truck window into the bed and then back in through the window, while doing roughly 80 miles per hour on the highway
3. Taunted a car full of black girls in the ghetto
4. Wore a jacket with a homemade back patch that said "Everyone is a cunt" to a feminist punk show
5. Lit my hair on fire numerous times
6. Shouted back at the cops who had us pinned against the wall beneath a bridge in Haverhill, MA
7. Challenged an anonymous woman threatening me with her shotgun
8. Fell off the train
9. Fell down the stairs and put my face through the wall at the bottom
10. Attempted to steal the entire PA I had found in the church basement while above me a hardcore show was underway
11. Etcetera, etcetera, etcetera

and today I was afraid of a chainsaw

22

All drugged up, out in the heat
Ready for a fight, ready for defeat

thicker than blood

23

1 PUNK point

Why piss on my parade

I'm having fun.....................................

25

DESTROY THE WORLD DESTROY
EVERYTHING

eing alone at night

I S   out of
        sight

the d a r k

e e r i e silence is

maddening in all its s
                      t
                       i
                        l
                         l
                          n
                           e
                            s
                             s

the dark static,
        making me manic
    insane   insane
      insane   insane
~~going~~ out of my brains   i luv it!

27

My Birthday—
today's my birthday, and
I sit alone in my library.
My brain ticks out regrets like
a printer.   I sit here and wonder

29

Gridlocked

```
    I  C  G
       A  E
       N  T
       N  O
       O  U
       T  T
```

ADD   Bipolar

psychosis is
in the eye of
the beholder
Skitzophrenia

Addict   OC

Why would I wanna be you?
  You're the one that's killing me

DO NOT
immitate
the hand that kills you

there's no **fun**

in

FUNDAMENTALISM

or is
    there

34

If you HANG OUT with

shitty people

you'll get shitty results

The things you say.... The things you do.... The lies you tell....

The people you screw....

YOU MAKE ME

SICK

the joke is broke
i look at the sky & some bloke
flips me the fuckin finger.
i open my mouth & fire
an insult flying back at him.
hits him in the face & i feel
i feel
I FEEL LIKE A FUCKIN GOD>>>

37

This is so very true:

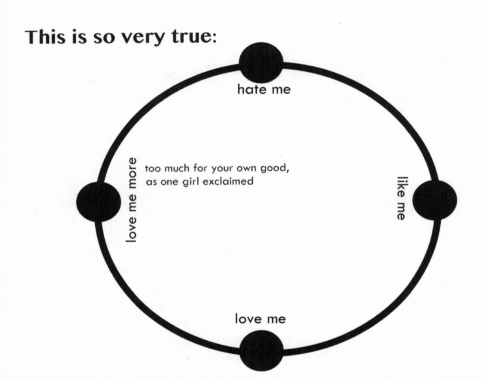

hate me

love me more

too much for your own good,
as one girl exclaimed

like me

love me

JADED eyes

40

If you play in filth
you'll
   come
      out
         dirty

If you clean up the filth
    you
       can
         focus
            on
               something else

Treading in the problem
will only get you

Do you really want me to stop
Do you really want me to stop
Do you really want me to stop

stop this.......

Is that really what you want...

Woud it really
make you happy????

Words are my weapon. If you piss me off, I will ~~murder you.~~ I COULD break it to you nicely, and I would. But if you piss me off, then ~~I won't.~~

I'm so ready to leave this place

I'm so ready to leave this place

I'm so ready to leave this place

I'm so ready to leave this place

leave this place

I'm so ready to

I just want to leave this Godforsaken place

Born in Boston, MA, Newton to be exact. Moved to Rutland, VT, maybe 5 years ago. Reside there for the time being, until I can get my shit together and move outta this bitch—once and for all

once and for all

Every girl I meet wants to fuck me, every guy I meet wants to fight me. I say things I regret but constantly tell myself I meant it. Stand strong and proud and turn the other cheek on your fellow man is my motto, and yet I'm so quick to help out the victim of persecution which I guess makes me a hypocrite, but a good hypocrite, a hypocrite who pushes negative vibes but acts nicely and kindly to everybody. I hate the nice me and wish to be the mean me but the truth of the matter is I couldn't hurt a fly, unless it bites me and then I will be the first to smash it dead. I'm a typical borderline case: I hate everybody but I'm always lonely and desperate for attention. I'm the first to tell you how much I love you, but deep down inside I hate you and want you dead, only if you died I'd miss you terribly, cuz what's the saying? Distance makes the heart grow stronger and fonder and I end up beating myself up (and off) until you're here and when I get you I toss you out the window hoping you land on your head. Ask Kristen, who I'm sure you know, all about it and she'll tell you she's been the victim of my insanity time and time again, but she loves me anyway and keeps coming back and I keep pulling her my way—except for one time, when she did the pulling for a change—and since she's so quick to forgive I feel she's my perfect girl-friend and I wanna marry her, unless I kill her first in which case I will cry and cry until I meet somebody else and then I forget all about her. A week passes and everybody's gone and I'm alone and beating myself black and blue at how stupid I was for destroying such a good thing. But soon af-ter, I find something else I can stick my dick into, stir it around like it's a pot of stew, pull it out, and shoot. That's my life. Welcome to hell!

45

I Love You

Which is why I've gotta cut off your head.

I hope you understand.

You look at my pictures
but you don't read my writing.
I've got something to say to you
but it always goes unread.

What am I to do
to make you care about my insides?
Should I put em on display
show myself from the outside in.

Would that make you care?
Seeing me hung up all bloody
my organs sliding out of my gutted stomach
and coiling on the floor beneath me.

At least then you'll see
there's more to me than
just a pretty face.
I got guts and a heart that pumps
and I got intestines and a brain that
races out of control at times.
It's all a part of me, all different sides,
but if you only look at my face
you won't see what I have to say.

do NOT fuck with me
NOT
NOT
NOT
N   O   T

ive done loads of crazy stuff. ive fallen off the subway train, i climbed out of a pickup truck window when the truck was doing 70 or 80 down the highway. i tried to steal the entire PA out of a church basement while a hardcore show was underway right upstairs, & I got caught red-handed by this big skinhead/hardcore kid who acted as a bouncer, & I had to book it—fortunately he never caught up w/ me because he wasnt the kind of guy who would call the cops.

ill admit it, im an alcohoholic/drug addict & i frequent AA meetings. see the thing is about alcoholics is they all live on the edge before they sober up. but me, as someone once pointed out, I had no edge to begin w/. there were no limits to my mayhem.

was it God who saved me? or was it jus pure luck? id like to think God & luck are one & the same. see, i dont pretend to know God because that would be a lie—make believe. what i do know is there is something beyond me, something which i may never come to understand because it is BEYOND ME. is this magical being pulling my strings, having saved me from my own self-destruction time & time again? i dont fucking know & i dont fucking care. it is what it is. now im here, today is not yesterday, nor is it tomorrow. today is today, & yesterday i soared in the clouds w/ vicious bats. tomorrow i might climb a mountain, but today this muse is shouting at me to create something worth viewing————————-sorry about my rant here.

I DID IT YOUR WAY

and failed

Yesterday   Today   Tomorrow

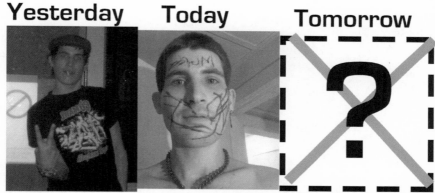

Another day, another crime. Another way, another rhyme.
Life happens and it happens and we become things we had
never expected to be, but we continue to grow and evolve
and become better and better men and women and one day
when we're looking death straight in the eye we realize we've
done it all and we're all ready to die..........

51

Life's not all bad

I suppose

There are plenty of things
to look forward to LIKE

like ... like ... like ... like

There are so many of them
I don't know where to begin

But you get the idea, I'm sure.......

53

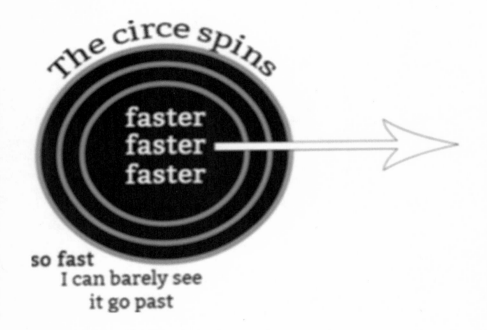

The circe spins

faster
faster
faster

so fast
I can barely see
it go past

RIOT

FUCKin

RIOT

The TV is exactly where it ought to be—bashed to pieces and chucked out the window.

Because **A BUSTED TELEVISION SET** is really a beautiful thing....

57

IN my old apartment
IN my old clothes
DAWNING that same
        devil-may-care grin on my face
WITH nothing useful in my head

NOTHING
HAS
CHANGED
in that
respect.

WILD
LIFE
(WE) ARE MERE
ANIMALS

Sometimes I feel so proud and smart that I just want to give myself a pat on the back. Other times I feel so hopeless and stupid that I just want to slam my head through a pane glass window. Sometimes I feel so full of joy that I want to walk down the street boasting and rubbing my happiness in the passersby's faces. Other times I feel so depleted that the existence of other people makes me feel as though they're boasting at **me,** rubbing their glee in **my** face, ramming it up my nose like it's a line of coke, etc. etc. etc.

Today's not one of those days.

People who have opinions are more selfish and egotistical than people who don't. Cuz people without opinions are saying, "I don't know." People with opinions are saying, "Well, I do know and let me tell you." I DON'T KNOW A GODDAMN THING ABOUT ANYTHING AND I AM SO PROUD OF THAT FUCKING FACT and you seem to know everything abut everything and are so proud of that fact. Fucking check your fucking ego, Mrs. Self-Righteous, Nose in the Air, Not-in-My-Backyard— I was about to say cunt, but I stopped myself because I know you're not a cunt, I know better than that. Just, no offense, your preaching is giving me a headache and I unfollowed you two days ago because of that, but you have the right to do it and I have the right to not listen.

LEAVE ME ALONE

cuz I can't hear you!!!

over your preaching....

61

Where do your actions fall?

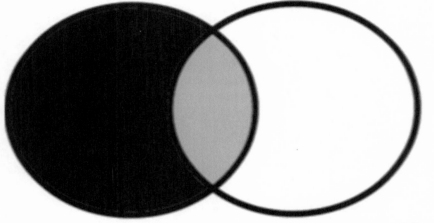

Pick one or be deemed immoral!

When every movement—even the smallest flexing of a muscle—requires a deep-seeded sigh, that's when you know something ain't right. You just lumber through life, a false sense of entitlement hovering over you, as if the world owes you something. A burden on everybody you've ever met, you sit alone in the dark and, when someone tries to spark a conversation with you, all you can say is, "I don't want to talk right now." You're a waste of space if you choose to carry on this way. Not to say you couldn't amount to anything, but your attitude (not your dillemna) *must* change first.

And, worst of all, you're really bumming me out!

Either
CHEER the fuck UP
or
KILL YOURSELF—— it'll save a lot of people the time & energy

When one door closes,
            another one opens. . . .
only I run thru too fast
slip on the black ice on the other side
crack my head on the pavement

What's worst. . . .
a dog moseys up to me
stop and cocks one hind leg
and fires a line of piss in my mouth

that's the kind of luck that I got

where you see strange
I see normal

where you see pain
I see enjoyment

where you see hate
I see love

where you see love
I see lust

you sick motherfucker

You're stupid
because
you're stupid 👉

Look at how cool I looked back in the day. Too bad, at 28-years old, I didn't retain any of the coolness. Quitting drugs will do that to you. Will strip away your cool. One moment you live your life like the nonchalant street demon you ought to be, and the next, having removed the heavy drug-using, you're a FUCKING nervous wreck.... The story of my life....

Was
looking at 5 to 10 years for
being in the wrong place, wrong time.
Came to Vermont as a way to evade the
jailtime hanging over my head, beat it by mere
seconds, and here I am, alive and well to tell you
my tale, a tale of fucking up, getting high, and
destroying EVERYthing.

And I do mean EVERYTHING

NO🚫 1

I'll scribble

LOVE

I will show you what it
means to be humiliated

all across your face
with my pretty knife

70

We were blood brothers

thicker than blood

71

See, I'm not just a hot piece of ass.

I know my shit. . . . . . .

I ENJOY

BEATING THE CRAP OUT OF

WOMEN

BECAUSE

IT MAKES ME FEEL

STRONG & POWERFUL

AND EVERYONE NEEDS TO FEEL

STRONG & POWERFUL

DON'T YOU JUDGE ME

It has nothing to do with
SPIKES
and
MOHAWKS
PAINTED LEATHER
CHAINS
and
TATTOOS

The fashion is irrelivant.

TAKE IT OFF

falling
falling
falling
falling
falling
falling
falling
falling
falling
falling
falling
falling

s
p
l
a
s
h

why not?????

First of all, ██████████. One thing that always helps me get in the swing of things is reading other people's writing. Or you could look at other modes of art and start with that. Also, about a year ago I started sleeping only every other night and I haven't had writer's block since. I only write the days after not sleeping, but on those days I write so damned much. I mean, I did 5 book in a year's time. I don't recommend not sleeping, though, cuz one of the side effects is for the past year I've been on an emotional roller coaster (which has been driving my writing very much so), and before I started this not sleeping spree, I had mellowed out tremendously.

I DREAM OF VIOLENCE

VIOLENCE

BUT
silence is
all I
ever get
in real
LIFE

I AM a MONSTER

and I will spit in your face

My dad wanted me to get the flu shot, was pushing me, pressing me, to get it. At the time I had a guy who at first I thought was a friend crashing with me, and he was big into conspiracy theories, believed in all sorts of whacky shit. When I told him I was going to get a flu show that afternoon, he said, No no no, blah blah blah, conspiracy theory, yadda yadda, they will get you, blah blah blah—BLAH. My dad who I trust for the most part, as I have known him way longer than this guy who at first I thought was a friend, seems to know his shit about these things, and this guy who at first I thought was a friend was discrediting my dad with his conspiracy babble. Honestly, I took it at first and just let him ramble but then, when he discredited my dad who I trust for the most part, stepped into the argument. I said, You know, there are two sides to every coin, two sides who flood the media with propaganda that will make you more likely to follow their side. And he said, No. So I said, This country was founded on propaghanda, you know. He said, No no. And I said, And it's up to the consumer to choose which side to believe in (which I must add is the reason I don't follow politics in the first place). He said, No, not true. There's only one way, this way, and it has to be that or I'll blow my fucking brains out all over the pavement (of course I'm adlibbing here). So I said, Where'd you get this so-called "information." And he said, There's so many places. I said, Name one. He said, I don't know where to begin. And so on....

And this guy claimed to be smart
Never trust those who claim to be smart

Something cheerful
something happy
not so low

I can do this, just let me think on it

for a minute

Being onstage gives me shivers
When I played in the band standing onstage
was remarkable, I had never felt a better joy
in the world.
Which is why today I frequent open-mikes.
to read my poetry.

Guess you could say
I get off on being the
center of attention.
Standing onstage and feeling
a thousand waiting, hopeful
eyes beaming at me—
nothing beats it.

How's that for positive?

82

The HARDest Decision I've Ever Had to Make

I love myself   I love myself not
I love myself   I love myself not

      People are starving
      dying

           getting raped
           and maimed.

Yet all I can think about
in this dire day & age
      is whether or not
         I love myself

              **It's the hardest decision
              I've ever had to make!**

I'm piecing the past back together

that's what I did this morning

sat at my computer looking thru my friends' friends on Facebook

so many

FAMILIAR FACES

who I just cannot place, even after thinking long and hard about it

it's kind of FRIGHTENING

and surreal to know that I know these people
I really do
but I just can't place them. . .

Crowd

Noise

Noise

Crowd

Crowd

Noise

V
o
i
c
e
s

Lonely

V
o
i
c
e
s

Crowd

Noise
Crowd

Crowd

Noise
Noise

Listening to the Drones. This band is sick. I just really got into them a few days ago and they're amazing and so damn catchy—when I'm not listening to them I still hear their songs in my head all day long.

Especially their song "Lookalikes."

"You lookalikes leave me alone / Don't wanna be like you / Emulate somebody you dont know // I don't wanna be like you / You don't wanna be like me / We don't wanna conform to you"

██████, no offense, but I don't care I don't care I don't care. My writing is getting better and better and better, and do you know why?—because I fucking love to write and writing loves me and I will do it regardless of whether you like it, because you're right, it's not about fame and acknowledgement, it's about the craft and I love every fucking bit of the craft. The fact that people enjoy my writing feels good and I can't deny it and I'm happy to know that people are reading it, but that's not why I do it, because IF that was why, I probably wouldn't do it because again, you are right, I am not a celebrity. And what's funny is, you've judged my writing on a very superficial basis because you've only seen the small glimpses of what I've posted here and you haven't delved into the longer stuff, the actual stories I've written that have characters I develop and move and bring to life. I USED to post longer stuff on Facebook but then I stopped because I realized if I want to sell books and get people interested—which is something I do want, in fact—I have to start with the simple and superficial stuff. So your comments above are superficial too and I don't care I don't care I don't care. I SIMPLY DON'T FUCKING CARE. I love to write and writing loves me and the fact that you don't like it doesn't change a thing!

I ——→ just ——→ don't ——→ care

I shat on a gravestone
this one time
the name on the stone was **POPE**
and then
since it was a veteran's graveyard
and there was an abundance of
American flags
I wiped my ass with an American flag
in broad daylight too
then a tiny lap dog stuck its head out   from behind the bushes
and I yanked my pants back on
and got shit all down my leg. . . .

CRAZY

shatter glass

chuck bricks

knock over gravestones

BURN

the American flag

BURN BURN BURN

BURN!!!

They will try and hold you down!

RISE ABOVE

You are better

You are stronger

You are faster

You are smarter

This world is filled with

 Cunts RISE ABOVE

92

ive fought w/ every oppressive force my entire life & ive always lost. im 28-years old & have fought-against since I was maybe 10. i realize now that im not a fighter, im a writer. everybody has a weapon of choice. my weapon is the written word. hopefully what i write will provoke action against various oppressive forces, but i doubt it. i dont partake in arguments because typically people are too unbendable to see another way of thinking. im the first to admit that im wrong. like, for example, that blog i wrote about feminists*—i was wrong about that, i acted on anger & not logic. im human and thats what humans do. most people, though, will do anything possible to not admit theyre wrong, so i dont bother argue. its not that im apathetic. its just that i have better things to do than scream at a wall. i do what i can to improve the world, but chances are im not going to incite a revolution.

*

I got mad at the facilitator of my weekly writers' group for cutting me off mid-poem because the content was "gross." So I went and wrote a blog to help me cope with my anger.

THE WORLD IS MY

. . . . candy store . . . .

and

I will never sell you my soul

sell out and be your whore....

life's too short for that anyway

94

Sometimes
the smartest people say
the stupidest things

Just now a woman told me the first time I met her I walked in to a crowded room full of people dressed fairly "normal," only my own style of dress was a bit out there—a torn shirt with a litter of safety pins holding it together, tight black jeans, and black spikey hair. She said I just walked in there without a care in the world, seemingly with no concern (or regard) for what anybody thought of me. I just walked in nonchallantly and lay down on the floor in front of everyone and spread out and made myself at home

I don't remember that specifically myself, but it does sound like something I may have done.

101

No respect…. No manners….

TROLLS I heard someone call them

As long as they remain anonymous
as long as they don't have a face

they can say just about anything to you

Thanks to social media, any idiot with a computer can voice
their opinions on just about any subject.

So now I'm getting reamed out by guys who couldn't
even write themselves out of a paper bag, who think
they have the merits to hassle me about my own writ-
ing.

I HAVE BEEN STUDYING
WRITING FOR YEARS....

But they don't care
But they don't care
But they don't care
But they don't care
But they don't care
But they don't care
But they don't care
But they don't care

You ask me
Are you an
narchist?

Fuck fuck fuck— I just saw this crazy cunt sucking a duck, so I said, What the? and went over and punched him in the nuts. He looked at me and grabbed his gun, said, Did you just whack me in the sack. He cocked his gat and put a 22-caliber right in my back.

105

Don't Tell Me About It

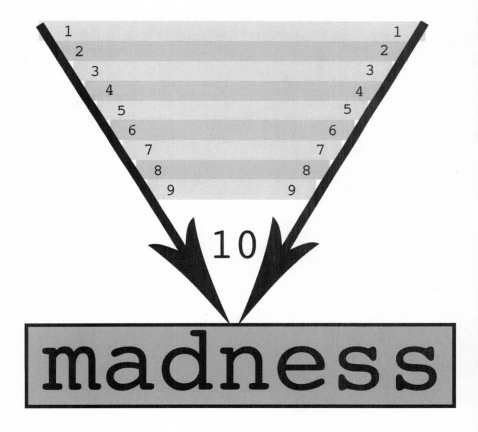

10

madness

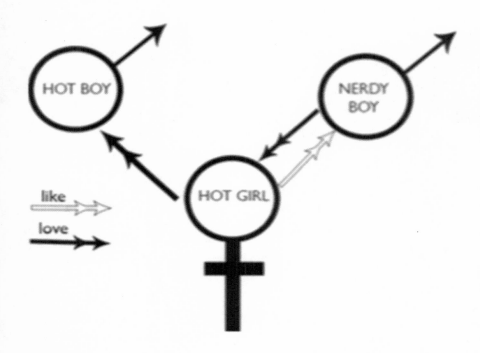

108

WHEN YOU'RE FEELING DOWN

I'll lift you up

WHEN YOU'RE FEELING UP

I'll knock you down

I'm just that kind of nice

feeling _____
(blank)

just got nothing

t   s
o   a
      y

guess I'm bored, just killing time
if you'd asked me why, I might have to say

I Don't Know

TOP SECRET

PHUcK

114

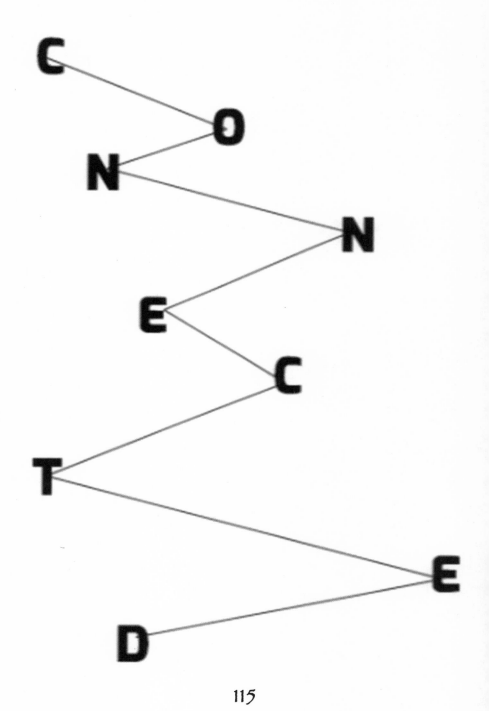

I'm a mongoloid

if that's	if that's
what you	what you
want to	want me to
believe	be

卐 |<u>RUN</u>| 卐

THE LAND OF THE FREE
is not free   at all

THE HOME OF THE BRAVE
is mostly populated by

P U S S I E S

The world that we know and love
        will most likely be nuked by
        terrorists.

HATE flourishes, whereas LOVE has died
                        many, many years ago

We think we're safe.
                But we're not.
                                Nobody is
                                        SAFE

The terrorists have won.
Our fate belongs to them.
                The terrorists have won.
                Get it through your head.

Now all we have left to do is .... |RUN|

117

i want freedom
i want freedom
i want freedom
i want freedom
i want freedom
i want freedom
i want freedom
i want freedom
i want freed
i want freed
i want frees

DON'T BE LIKE THEM!!!

CONF-
ORM

Anti–

EVERYTHING

Nobody is

SAFE

This fucking guy

WHO CLAIMED TO BE AN ANARCHIST
I must add

accused me of being a Nazi because of my dark art

and because I said everyone

> I disapprove of what you say, but I will defend to the death your right to say it.

FROM ALL WALKS OF LIFE

has the right to express themselves whichever way they choose.

So this fucking guy

WHO CLAIMED TO BE AN ANARCHIST
I must add

threatened to stomp my face in....   via Facebook, no less

My response: I'll be looking forward to tasting the bottom of your boot, then.
His response: You don't have to taste it if you would just stop producing this "propaganda."
My response: See, I'd rather taste the bottom of your boot than be censored like that.

And this was thus followed by a completely uncalled-for volley of threats.

When a man breaks his legs he has to acknowledge this fact and use crutches to aide him in walking until he can walk on his own again. He can surely deny this fact and try and walk on his own anyway, without the help of crutches, but that won't get him very far. Plus, his legs won't ever heal and he'll forever be a prideful gimp.

THINK ABOUT IT

PLEASE
DON'T
LOCK
ME
UP!!!

I am a NARCISSIST

I'll be the first to admit it

 **BUT I'M NO DIFFERENT**

than you!

....ain't it true....

Video games are so fucking lame. If I was going to compete against you with my thumbs, I'd much rather have a butt picking contest. Because then at least we'll come out with some real shit.

Hahahahahahaha

126

I wanna stay young & fresh

as oppose to old &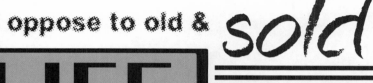

doesn't sound like
much of a life to me

I want to create life, as oppose to waste life

I want to live
I don't want to die

not yet, anyway

127

Punk to me has always been about the MISFITS banding together.

What's more MISFIT than saying something against the mass majority?

I've gotta survive

somehow

130

It's a new day, only new is no longer in my vocabulary. The same old same old, yawn!, boring, old news, blah blah blah. I should hire someone to stick me in the ass with a hot poker everytime I get stagnant. Just a poke, and I'll leap forward and yodle as loud as my lungs can take. It'd keep life interesting, or painful. Interesting *and* painful.

The only guy friend who ever gave me head

thicker than blood

132

BE YOURSELF

BE YOURSELF

BE YOURSELF

BE YOURSELF

BE YOURSELF

135

136

spinning spinning spinning spinning spinning spinning spinning

stretched

stacked	stacked
stacked	stacked
stacked	stacked
stacked	stacked
stacked	stacked
stacked	stacked
stacked	stacked
stacked	stacked

a polliticaly corect PUNK? ive never herd a such a thing. i thought Punk rawk was foundid on the absence of corect ANYthing. i meen, theres Richard Hell (& he was tha first) who walked tha streets of New York City wearing a t-shirt sed "Pleeze Kill Me," w/ a bulseye in tha senter.   Darby Crash who died his hair blu to see wat it wud be like to be the only nigger in an all wite skool.

shall i go on?

Sid Vicious wearing tha swastika
Minor Threat saying "Guilty of Being Wite"
Tha Lewd w/ there song "Kill Yerself"
Tha Forgotten Rebels & TSOL both
    saying they wud rather fuk tha ded....

shall i go on....

SCREAM
FOR
freedom

I'm outta my mind
            outta my head
i don't understand what you say
        It don't matter what I said

I'm one of a kind
            be better off dead
It don't matter what I say
        cuz I'm outta my head

LOSE CONTROL

My skull is hard
            my brain is mush
I can't get a grip
    but who said I want a grip????

My skin is scarred
            my heart is squished
I can't get a grip
            cuz my dick is limp

R I P

The Present

Love sucks. Hate is great.
Better destroy your love before it's too late.
If you love, you will lose.
I'd much rather be sniffing glue.
My past proves this all the same,
that love will bring me down and drive me insane.
Beside I got nothing I care to share.
Love love love,
it'll tear up my heart and leave me bleeding to death.
Why bother when it hurts so damn much????

Because it's worth the fuss....

144

ideology = idiocracy

146

G E T   I T   S T R A I G H T

ALL THE SHIT I POST ON FACE-
BOOK, UNLESS STATED OTHER-
WISE, IS TOTALLY ORIGINAL

BUT PEOPLE PROBABLY SEE IT
AND THINK I'M JUST ONE MORE
RIP OFF ARTIST IN THIS WORLD

that I'm merely stealing other people's art and other peo-
ple's words, just like the Internet was designed for *as if*

ALTHOUGH I DO ENJOY RIPPING PEOPLE OFF
I'm not in the same class as the mass majority
of people who lack creativity

147

Act Your Age

Grow Up   Act Your Age

Two Phrases I Never Really Cared for When I
Was a Kid

All That Time when people barked jeremy when
are you gonna grow up I **Was** Acting My Age.
Just the Thing Is, They Were All Just in Too
Much a Rush to Grow Up Themselves, on the
run from their own ages. but you see, for me, I
Didn't Care Too Much about What Others
Thought or Felt and Feeling That Way Was Quite
Disinhibiting, as if i had inhibitions to begin
with, which i didn't. i was satisfied with my own
immaturity, i was fine with being a Kid for a few
more years, because growing up and holding
down the same job day in, day out seemed quite
the boring life and I Wanted None of It

no wonder you hate me
you didn't believe me
                when I said
        PROCEED WITH CAUTION

                                    im wild &
                                        free
                            running with
                                SKUNKS

the lesson here   CAUTION
    is
    DO NOT do   CAUTION
    what you're told   CAUTION

DON'T LISTEN   c a u t i o n

this guy I knew
sed it first   join us!

It will blow your mind

GET ME OUT OF HERE

150

From little runt to hardcore Punk train hopping street vermin beggar.
What happened????

For most men aging means adding depth and maturity to their overall look, but for Henry the Barbarian, formerly known as Henry Albert, aging means just the opposite.

From being a little runt of a high schooler, riding a skateboard around and smoking pot, to a nihilistic crusty Punk who spends his days behind a cardboard sign asking people for spare change, and his nights inside a bottle.

Hero or Vagrant?

I have ideas
big fucking ideas
        DREAMS REALLY
        IF YOUD WISH TO NAME IT SOMETHING
~~But the thing is~~   I promise you, this claim is
                           not me self-depricating, nor
~~the problem is~~   is it an excuse for my lack
                           of success in life....
~~the truth of the matter is~~   ....it's true....
                                      is all....
        IM JUST A LAZY SLOB
~~Im just too damn apathetic~~ TO ACCOMPLISH ANYTHING

155

I JUST DON'T KNOW!!!

Destroy	Destroy	Destroy
Your LIFE	Your FAMILY	Your FRIENDS
KILL	THEM	ALL

157

Love
Lust
Love
Lust

You can run

but you can't hide

i'm comin' for you

DELVE

160

thicker than blood

Make guns not love for America

Hated and Proud

Anarchy

Anti-archy

Anti-hierarchy

No Government

No governing forces

No rules, no laws, no limitations

Stop calling yourself an anarchist!!!!

162

Punk rock has always been my escape from the oppressive 9-to-5 world we live in, my much-needed release that came at the end of every week, where I could see my friends, and a badass band would play, and the crowd would go wild. We'd swirl in front of the stage, feet kicking, fists swinging, knees pumping, elbows thrashing. We'd spin. We'd crash and burn, fall to the ground and get lifted up just to be hurled back into the madness. When I was a kid, those were the best times of my life. Taking out all that pent-up aggression in the form of moshing was the greatest thing in the world. Nothing mattered when I was in the pit. Not the girl who rejected me on Monday, the job that fired me on Tuesday, the teacher that failed me on Wednesday, my parents telling me I'm grounded on Thursday, or the big kid that beat me up on Frida—none of it fucking mattered when I was in the pit.

The Middle Child Strikes Again

I grew up in a dog family.
Everyone in my family has a dog.
That includes my inner family (my mom & dad, my bother,
    and my sister; EVERYONE)
and my outer family too.

                                      But me, I have a cat.

I grew up in a family of goodie-two-shoeses.
Everyone in my family followed the rules.
Sure, there were the slight bouts of drinking
                  the occasional experimentation.
But still—mostly it was
        good grades
        good marks
        good students.

                                    But me, I was bad.

Nor does anyone smoke cigarettes.
Nor is anyone diagnosed with symptoms.

I could go on forever.
But the fact of the matter is   I'm just different.

CASE CLOSED

165

N N N

morals   values   conscience

I've got NOTHING

4 U

I looked like Sid Vicious—not intentionally (well, maybe a bit intentionally). And I acted like Darby Crash, said everyone I knew back in my Punk rock glory days—also not intentionally.

Although people used to give me shit saying I was trying to act like Stiv Bators or Sid Vicious or Darby Crash, when really I was just being myself.

Not my fault Punk rockers who died way before I was even born acted like ME. I wasn't going to change the way I acted so that I wouldn't fit a silly Punk rock cliché. It's just the way it is, you know.

Another
DEAD
Freak

Another Lost

SOUL

is coming 4

YOU

169

I'm a mess

Come and join me

dot dot dot dot dot dot dot dot

I feel like a king

feel so cool

I AM LOST

170

and I have the right

call me whatever you want
it don't change a goddamn thing

BE BLUNT

SPEAK YOUR MIND

SHOOT FROM THE HIP

i encourage it....

CENSOR NOTHING

let the people decide what is real

173

Nothing Nothing Nothing
Nothing Nothing Nothing
Nothing Nothing Nothing
Nothing Nothing Nothing
Nothing Nothing
Nothing Nothing
Nothing Nothing
Nothing Nothing
Nothing Nothing Nothing
Nothing Nothing Nothing
Nothing Nothing Nothing
Nothing Nothing Nothing
Nothing Nothing Nothing
Nothing Nothing Nothing

I am Jeremy Void
because
I am Jeremy Void
because
I am Jeremy Void

Scattered
Scattered
Scattered
Scattered
Scattered
Scattered
Scattered
Scattered
Scattered
Scattered
Scattered

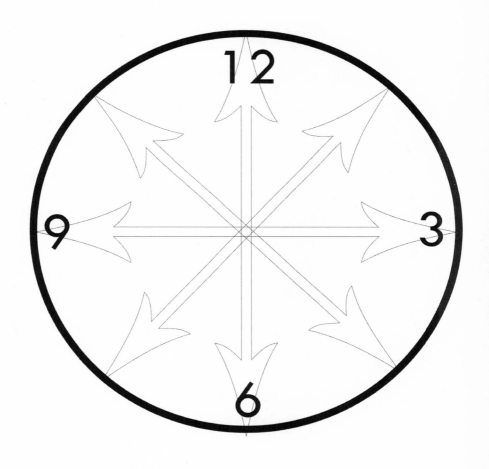

178

Everyone's so politically correct and I'm sick of it

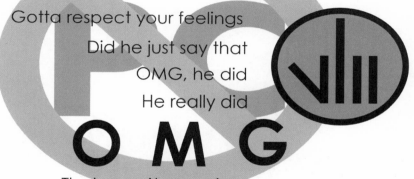

Gotta respect your feelings

Did he just say that

OMG, he did

He really did

OMG

That wasn't very nice

Say you're sorry

179

180

OF
T
H
O
U
G
H
T

They want me to change
say the way I live my life
is detrimental to
        the lives around me.

So now I've gotta change.
But nobody specified in what ways.

THE THING IS I have changed.
    A LOT
My perspectives of the world
my atitudes toward the world
my desires and disinclinations too.

So sorry I'm not your spitting image
        of perfection.

If I could be any letter in the
alphabet, it would be:

I would be goth too if my mom killed herself and my dad beats me cuz he said it's all my fault. If my girlfriend chained me up and forced me to watch while she fucks some other guy. Or if I had no balls and liked to bitch and moan and complain about everyone being mean and nobody liking me and boo hoo my life sucks so I'm gonna go and dress in black and tell every-one how bad it is because they just have no idea what it's like to be me—boo hoo!

HEY GOTH

FUCK OFF

Love = a shot of cocaine, the feeling of the drug rushing your veins, the pow when the madness hits you in the brain, that part when you feel oh so happy and you're never gonna fall, and then it leaves your system and you drop drop drop into a pit of despair where the only relieve is another hit of the thing that brought you here

you just have no idea ...

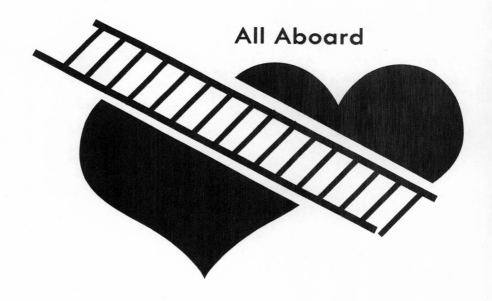

All Aboard

panic>>>>   My mind races,
                    my heart chases its own
                          tail ITS OWN TAIL
My eyes dart around the coffee shop
futily searching but not stopping on
A N Y T H I N G.

                        Nerves rapid-firing

signals flying through my veins
but not catching on . . . . .

                         |I'm scared|!
                         I'm scared !

The torment I put myself through
I should never have come here
voices shouting too loudly in my ears

   My head throbs as if
                    a thick ring of radiation
                          pulsates within. . . . .

I JUST CAN'T TAKE IT

ANYMORE

Who Are You?
To Tell Me
WHAT TO DO

I met a girl who liked to talk a lot and complain even more. First thing she said to me was, I hate the government, they suck. And I listened to her, I really did. You punk kids really have no idea how bad the government actually is, about what they do and stuff. You wouldn't even believe me if I told you. I have insider information. You can't buy this kind of information. I said, But you work at Walmart (she does work at Walmart). And she said, Well I need the money. So I'm thinking, What a freaking whore, letting the government rape her, as she claims they RAPE people, for some cash to buy her booze and cigarettes. Doesn't make much sense, you know. Eventually, when I grew tired of her bitching and moaning about the bad bad government, I said, What's so bad about the governemt? She stopped there and stared at me, probably perturbed that I had challenged her like that. Yeah, I said. What's so bad about the government? And she said, There's so many things bad about it. I said, Name one. She said, I don't know where to begin. And so on...

And this girl claimed to be smart
Never trust those who claim to be smart

TONIGHT
we're gonna
fuck shit up

LET'S
fuckin do it!

How does that make you feel?

It makes me feel bad, doc.

Huh.

What am I gonna do, doc?

Huh.

Doc, I need help.   Help, doc.   Help.   Help   Help.

H e

**And how does that
make you feel?**

l *p!*

Fucking **BAD**

I see. I'm getting a new

doctor **How does that make you feel?**

192

i will

Fuck
Facebook

It will suck your face out thru your
eyes and nail it to a cross.

Reduce you to a mere photograph. And all your
so-called "friends" to blank entities with the the
personaity of a series of memes.

I know, it happened to me

Hatred is Purity

195

A LITTLE PIECE OF MY INSANITY

I don't want to hate anymore. Only I can't stop hating. What I do want is love. Only I can't start loving. What I need is somebody, to tell you the truth. Somebody who will spit on me and put me down. What I need is you to punish me. What I want is for you to go away. But while you're here, you might as well punch me, kick me, hit me with all you got. Spit on me, humiliate me. Make me feel pain, it's what I need. I want you to leave me be, but you have no idea what it means to be me, and if you did, you might just hurt me, throw dirt on me, kick me around and make me bite the fucking curb. What I need, what I want, it's all the same in the end. Just make me know pain. It's the only way.

Everything I Say Is Wrong, Everything I Do Is Wrong. All I Want Is Wrong. All I Need Is Wrong. My Whole Existence Is Wrong and It's Burning a Hole in My Heart. I Just Want to Be Right, but at What Cost Is Being Right? What's It Worth Because I Know for Me Being Right Means Being Even More Wrong Than Before, so I Take My Heavy Head and I Beat It Against the Wall until I Bleed and then Look Straight into the Mirror and Ask Myself What Is Wrong with Me, and I Say Through Missing Teeth, Everything.... And Jerk My Head Back and Let A Loogie Fly and Splatter in My Own Fucked-up, Bloody Face.

Confused
Disorganized
Dissheveled

197

stop yelling at me please stop I dont deserve this kind of treatment I don't deserve to be treated this way youre hurting my ears stop it Im doing the best I can and with your senseless yelling how can you possibly expect me to do any better stop yelling stop please please just tell me what I did to you tell me how I hurt you please just stop yelling at me or Im gonna lose it I swear Im gonna lose it if you dont stop please stop Im gonna lose it Im gonna lose it Im gonna lose it

Im gonna lose it
Im gonna lose it
Im gonna lose it

please why wont you shut UP!

EVERYTHING IS BROKEN
EVERYTHING'S A JOKE
THE CAUSTIC MIRROR
LOOKS BACK AT ME

and I hate the faces
that it makes....

COME ON DOWN

AND

JOIN THE RIDE

will   your

you   lose   MIND

Punk rock has a very sacred place in my heart. So when I see someone dressing Punk because it looks cool, forgive me for wanting to smash their face in!

NO NO NO NO NO, EVERYTHING I WRITE HAS BEEN SHIT LAST NIGHT AND I CAN'T SEEM TO GET IT RIGHT AND I'VE BEEN WRITING SO WELL FOR SO LONG AND IT SEEMS LIKE IT WOULD NEVER END, BUT I THINK IT'S COMING AND IT'S COMING, FUCKING WRITER'S BLOCK, AND IT'LL SHATTER MY HEART...

FUCK ME, IT'S STARTING....

If my mind don't kill me
my body will

I'm an artist.
    I'm lazy and weak.
I'm an artist,
    whose past was crazy
        and whose future is bleak

It's not my imagination, there's a gun on my back.
My neighbors are packing heat
staring at me with their beady eyes.
My teachers talk about me in the teacher's lounge.
I know they do.   I know they do.
There's no way to   deny it.
Cops eyeing me down when I cross them on the street.
Children gawking at me like I'm some kind of
freak.
Then there are my peers
always conspiring against me
planning to undermine me
to take me in the shower and
fuck me.

All the fucking torment
the torment they put me through.

I know they want me dead. I know they want me dead.
I just know it.
Well what are you waiting for?
What are you fuckng waiting for?

Kill me already!!!

Total Take Over

✓ ✓ ✓ ✓ ✓ ✓ ✓ ✓

I'm doing great. Living the nightmare, and trying to find ways to market that. I wanna exploit the exploiters, steal money from the rich and burn it all to the ground. Just pile it up, douse it in gasoline, light a match, and let the flame do the rest. I wanna see the sociopathic big business men fall to their knees and ball as they watch their children perish amid billows of cigarette smoke and piles of fast food. I wanna witness the world turning in on itself, the poor getting rich and fat, and the rich getting skinny on crack. One of these days I'll turn water to wine. Treat the poor to a drink while the rich stand on the corners panhandling for our easily swindled dough. And then I'll be doing better than great, I'll be grand, I'll feel like the man, and my ego would have skyrocketed, and in a few years the rich will rise the ranks and knock me down and take all my cash and force me to work as a gizz catcher at the local strip club. Every man will have their day.

✓ ✓ ✓ ✓ ✓ ✓ ✓ ✓

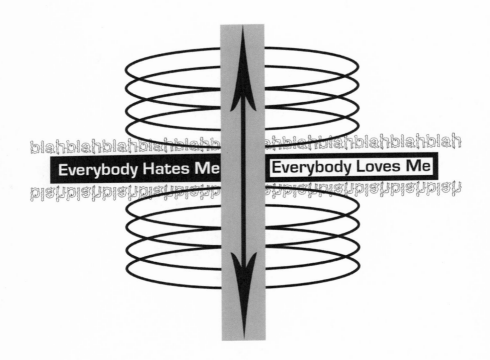

206

I AM

SELFISH

I ONLY WANT

TO HELP

Haven't listened to the Business in a long, long time. Last show I saw in Boston was the Business, and I got blitzed. Drank over 100 dollars in beer, and people bought me drinks left and right cuz I claimed to have just gotten out of prison. At one point during their set these two girls heard my knee snap over the music and ran in the pit and dragged me out and set me against the wall. Then "Guiness Boys" came on and I shoved them both out of the way and did a swan dive right back into the fucking moshpit. The next day, I swear my bone was sticking out my knee.

GOOD TIMES

You wouldn't believe all the good I do
            on a day-to-day basis
            probably more than you
                  when it comes down to basic tactics.

But I don't promote it
I don't paint myself as a saint
because that would defeat the purpose
                  now, wouldn't it?

Painting myself as a villain
seems much more saint-like
                  if you ask me.
Masking the good with sinister things
making you seem like the asshole
            goes to show
            just how purely selfless I am.

But let the record be straight
                  here
                        now
that I'm only telling you this because
            I feel it must be said
            so that you know
            I'm not such a bad individual after all
            but a selfless individual with
            a twisted sense of humor.
Really
**I'm just trying to give you a mirror
            into yourself**   is all. . . .

Addict

Ambitions

I Can't Draw

I Can't Draw

I Can't Draw

I Can't Draw

I Can't Draw

I Can't Draw

PERIOD

Everybody

and that means you....

is doing the best they can

with the knowledge they think they know

Smash up

yOuR

knowledge

before it defeats you

So

in **L**ove with

Enticed by

Wowed

Dumbstruck

4 **U**

213

CREATING

i

CAN'T

STOP

CREATING

this goddamn

MUSE

will not leave me alone

We'll do just what we wanna do

Get out of our way

we're the wrecking crew

I suppose I don't know what it's like
to be you
I suppose I never lived a day
in your shoes
But not to sound grandiose or anything
I lived through hell
and if you only knew the hell that I know
you might reasses your stance
Trust me on that

QUOTE THIS:

After this one
I'm calling it
quits..................
Im done
finished
and I mean it this time
SuRELy I dO

Just like the last time

218

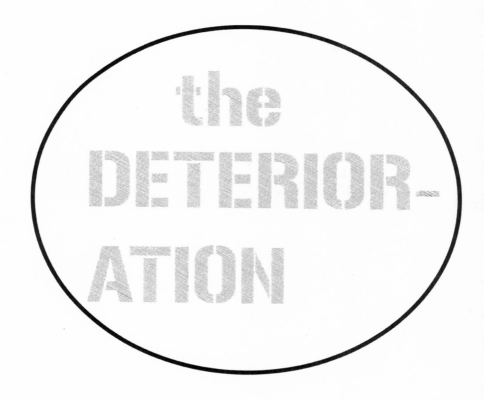

the DETERIOR-ATION

i've got a thought disorder
my thoughts are in disorder

It's OVER
and now I'm sad....

The Punk scene has become a cesspool for politicians and winey, ball-less liberals who would much rather preach to you than put their head through a wall. Me, I'd rather put my head through a wall. Or moreover, I'd rather put the preacher's head through a wall.

When I say politicians, I don't mean anarchists, as an anarchist politician is a bit of a paradox, don't you think? Punk to me has always been an anti-politic, THE anti-politic. I considered myself an anarchist when I was a kid but then changed my views as I grew older because I realized anarchy in and of itself is in fact a paradox. Although I still share some anarchist points of view, I started considering myself a nihilist, well kinda—I believed in chaos, in ultimate freedom: "Censor censorship" became my slogan, along with, "Everyone is a cunt"; and I realized there was something very wrong with the world, only I didn't know what it was. I was a hypocrite, a junky, a cretin, and a thief, but that was okay because I'd rather be a villain than one of "them." Something was wrong, I was wrong, you were wrong, but that's okay because I'd rather be "wrong" than "right" because "right" represented everything I was against. Punks aren't freedom fighters trying to incite a revolution; they are kids just like me and you trying to survive in an oppressive world that will not stop until our culture has been diffused. I don't want change because every option we have been presented with is all the same; they all reek of neglect and disgust. I want something that has yet to be discussed. Something new. Something better. I want the freedom to be me, is all.

YOU DO WHAT YOU WANNA DO
I'LL DO WHAT I WANNA DO

Turn the page →

{Stark}

SHRINKING

DIGRESSING

LOSING MY HEAD

THINGS ARE MOVING
AND THEY'VE NEVER MOVED
QUITE LIKE THIS BEFORE

⬇ (continue at your own risk) ⬇

225

I MELT
I MELT
I MELT

MY EYES BULGE OUT
CHILDREN RUN AT THE
SIGHT

OF IT

THE EARTH HAS FLIPPED

around

and Im scaaaaaaared————MUTANTS ARE SWARMING
the streets

↓ (continue at your own risk) ↓

226

RUN AWAY

FROM ME

Like Screaming at a Wall

like

screaming

at

a wall

aaaahhh

Someday
it's *gonna*
FALL

Turn the page ➔

Contained

233

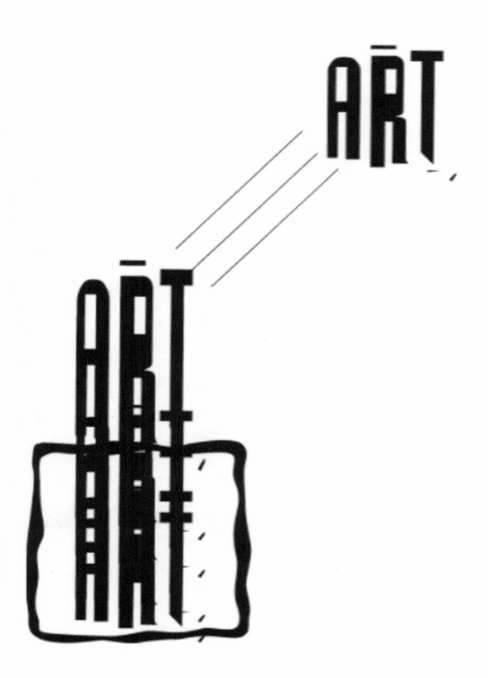

234

Turn the page

Her name is JenN

236

Her name is JenN

The strangest thing happened tonight
^^^^^^

really fuckin strange.

I met **s o m e o n e** who reminded me so so so much of someone I once knew—someone who I held very dearly
and

VERY CLOSE TO MY HEART

so Strange....

Her name was Jen **n**

with two Ns, **she made sure to point out.**

This one girl I dated for nearly ten years—ON AND OFF, of course, FOR NEARLY 10 YEARS—you know the one—her name is Kristen—and I'm so in love with her.

237

This older woman I met tonight was like an older version of Kristen—my one and only true love.

She shared that same energy Kristen always seemed to possess, never taking anything serious—for the first fifteen minutes after meeting this woman everything she said was a lie   —a lie

Then when I took a closer look I noticed she kind of even resembled Kristen, in a way—granted, it was a bit of a stretch.

She even bought
my sampler.

Then I saw my friend BJ—he came in right before I read— and without even thinking of saying goooodbye I took off with BJ and went to the bar next door—shortly, though, as I left that place soon after.

As I was walking home
HALFWAY HOME
I realized I left my iPad at Pub 42

and IT WAS BRAND-NEW
too.

238

So I double-backed to the bar, hurried through the door, and snatched it from the same spot on the floor beside the microphone where I had left it—   still there!

I passed Jen**n** on my way out, waved goodbye, and hurried back the way I'd come—back home.

But she screamed:

WAIT!

I stopped there, just outside the door,
and she ran to me
straight-up <u>ran</u>
    and then she <u>embraced</u> me
        like the way Kristen might
        embrace me, tight and firm

      and sensual—for one minute
        and then another
        and then another
        and then she released me

and I walked home....

Parental Advisory

PARENTAL

ADVISORY

Your kids are learning to swear from the TV, from their friends at school   Your kids are learning to swear from **YOU**

PARENTAL

ADVISORY

**You can't monitor them
forever**

Turn the page ➤

ART

ART

I'm a writer, I'm an artist. I like to delve into dark

subjects, explore and fuck them, dissect them and

poke and prod at their veins until a vessel bursts

and blood sprays in my face, to show me

I've hit the spot!

but, you see

I

AM

NOT

CRAZY....

I can assure you of THAT

245

I portray those twisted subjects so well because I am no more than a very talented fucking writer. It's what I do, and

it's what I do best....

THE BEST KIND OF ART, in my opinion,

is ART THAT

ART THAT SNAPS AT YOU

GROWLS AND BARKS AND GRITS ITS VICIOUS fucking TEETH AT YOU

THAT'S MY KIND OF ART

Art that lacks angst

... well ...

isn't art at all

I'm so sorry if my work
offends you....
Didn't mean it
like that....

I'm so sorry if my work
pisses you off
makes you vomit
scares you gay
because although that would be

I didn't mean it like that....

The way you choose to
perceive my work is on you....

I'm just the Artist

Trash

250

To you

I AM

TRASH

To me
YOU ARE
TRASH

Relativity
defines
perspective

BOTTOM LINE

Swearing Loudly

SWEARING LOUDLY

At a nearby Panera Bread two boys are swearing loudly, goofing off, doing what boys do, really, but to the surrounding families in the vicinity, they look like assholes and this must be stoppppped. The father of two girls doesn't want to hear the curse words even though at work with his racist coworkers he swears and puts down faggots. He puts them down good.

But not around his kids. His Kids. His innocent little girls who do not get exposed to it by their own friends at school or even by their own bigoted father who curses out spics and niggers when he talks to his mistress over the phone unaware that his two daughters are playing SPY games and absorbing every word he uses from the next room over.

So what does he do?——he rises to his feet with a deep-seeded sigh and then marches over to the two boys' table, a righteous feeling hovering over him like a halo. He stops at the boys' table, folds his arms in front of him, and fake-coughs. The boys look at him.

The one on his right looks back at his friend and says, "Who's this asshole?"

His friend shrugs and the two boys resume like the father wasn't even there.

The father tries one more time to get their attention, but they ignore him.

So the father drives his fist into the table, a powerful maneuver loaded with 2 tons of construction-worker force, and with a reverberating clunk the table rattles radically. The boys look at him, and now, finally, they're scared—or maybe just a little.

What the father doesn't know, doesn't realize in his uncalled-for rage, is that all the occupants of Panera Bread have his attention too.

"You little twits," he barks. "I'm here with my freakin' kids trying to have a nice time when yous are over here swearin' like sailors. If I hear one more freakin' swear come out of either of you boys' mouths, I will lift yous up and drag yous outside and kick the crap out of both of you. You think I'm kidding?"

Both boys shake their heads.

"Good!" the father says, and turns and walks away. The whole dining room opens up in applause.

The boys leave shortly after.

Turn the page

God, Are You Out There?

God, Are You Out There?

WHY AM I HERE?
AM I HERE?
AM I HERE?

I'VE GOTTA GET OUT
GOTTA GET OUT
GOTTA GET OUT
OF HERE RIGHT NOW

WHAT'S THE POINT?
I NEED TO KNOW
GOD, ARE YOU OUT THERE?
PLEASE GIVE ME
THE ANSWERS!

IF YOU DON'T
IF YOU CAN'T
IF YOU WON'T
TELL ME THE ANSWERS

THEN I DON'T KNOW
GUESS THIS SHOTGUN LOOKS NICE
AGAINST MY HEAD
FITS NICE AND FIRM
NICE AND LOVELY

259

AND I BET IT WILL BLOW
QUITE A BEAUTIFUL HOLE
WHICH WILL BRING ME CLOSER TO

THE ANSWERS I SEEK

**God, please
I'm begging you to answer
me....**

ARE YOU OUT THERE

Turn the page ➜

(Garamond, Pt. 14, 6" x 9", 1"/0.5" Margins)

Why are you so mad at me

What did I e v e r do to you

Listen to me   please

Stop talking   and
       listen

For fucks sake   **I**
                                  am
                              Jeremy   *Void*

I am not crazy
I am not selfish

I am not lazy
Nor am I   a fucking hellion

                              I
                              am
                          Jeremy   *Void*

Stop yelling at me
Stop your senseless
           ranting & raving

I dont deserve this kind of treatment

I dont deserve this shit

STOPPIT
PLEASE, stoppit

Stop   Stop   Stop
Stop Stop Stop Stop Stop Stop Stop Stop Stop Stop

and
leave me
alone

                    if you know what's good for you!

P L E A S E

Turn the page ➔

Camping Trip

Camping Trip

THIS STORY

is 100% true

You might not believe it
might call me a liar
tell me to stop projecting
these feelings only come from
your inner perceptions of yourself.

Anyway

Last weekend I attended a retreat that was being
held by a certain support group I attend fre-
quently. I heard one guy at the meetings, who re-
minds me so much of my older brother (has a lot of

267

the same mannerisms and stuff), talk about this all-men's camping trip; it's a real happening event, he would say in his own words.

I thought, Why not? I was coming up on one-year sober from drugs and alcohol, and doing fairly well, better than ever in fact, so I thought, Why the fuck not? I approached this guy I've never had a real conversation with because of those stupid mannerisms and my own traumatic past (that's projecting; see, I know my shit) and said, I'd go, but I don't exactly have a ride. He'll drive me, he volunteered. Okay, I said. Later I would give him the whole thirty-five dollars to reserve myself a campsite.

And it happened right on schedule, last weekend; I just got back yesterday afternoon.

Throughout the retreat we had 12 speakers speak about their recovery from drugs and alcoholism—the seriousness of their infliction, what they did to put a plug on it, and how their life is different (better) now. The last guy to speak told this story about how he arrived at a meeting with his brother and upon entering the place he spotted a really rugged-looking biker guy with scarred and tattooed skin wearing an old, worn leather jacket. When his brother said, Where do you wanna sit? this guy telling us the story, he pointed to the man and said, There, all because the man looked as though he could use a friend, could use some good old-fashion recovery in fact. Turned out he was the speaker for that meeting and had a lot of time under his belt.

What's funny about this is that guy speaking didn't exchange a single word with me the whole time I was there, except for a passing, mumbled goodbye when it was time to leave.

Not a whole lot of guys spoke to me, either.

There were

Adam (the guy who reminds me of my older brother, and who drove me there), **Ben** (the guy who helped Adam drive up there with all the gear since he had a truck and Adam's car was jam-packed to its limit without the gear in it, and who let me chill in his pickup truck all of Friday night because there was a major hurricane-like rainstorm), *Andrew* (who shared Ben's and Adam's and my campsite, and whose tent I slept in the only night I did go to sleep), and **Mike** (who approached me before breakfast—or was it lunch?—and said he wasn't much of a people person either, told me he used to write poetry after I told him I'm a writer, and allowed me to read him some of my work), and then there were the guys who approached me, said a few words, and wandered off; and oh yeah, there was *Phil* as well, only because he too lived in Rutland so we had that in common and plus he had to give me a ride home since Adam had picked up a another passenger.

There were

30 CAMPERS

in attendance.

We were given a long break on Saturday afternoon— a good five to six hours — and I found myself staring at the empty pavilion we had been occupying, because everyone left without me, to go to Manchester and grab lunch; or to go here, there, somewhere, anywhere———

They weren't serving lunch at Emerald Lake State Park because there was no one there to cook it....

I WAS ALONE
BY MYSELF
A LITTLE PISSED BUT NOT TOO MUCH

WHEN OUT OF NOWHERE Phil COMES UP TO ME AND SAYS, IM GOING FISHING WANT A RIDE DOWN TO THE LAKE?

So, long story short, I ended up sitting on the beach by myself for a good five to six hours—I got the sun burns to prove it; guess I should have used sun block——staring at all the smoking hot MILFs

and writing poetry and creating ART in my

notebook. I watched people, internally laughed when they did something stupid, and even witnessed a loud, maybe a little bit out of control domestic dispute between three teenagers, one boy and two girls.

The boy was s p a z z i n g out, completely.

So, all and all, I kept myself fairly entertained.

But was I mad?

Not yet.

It didn't really hit me until the last speaker spoke and said how he is all about greeting the new-comer who's the least social in the group, regard-less of how scary or weird they look, because the program teaches that everyone is allowed in.

Except me.

So I got thinking. . . . . . .

After the last speaker we went around and said what we were grateful for and a lot of people said they were grateful that everyone was so accept-ing———and <u>that's</u> when it hit me!

One guy was near tears because he was so happy. Me, I don't cry when I'm happy, never have and

274

probably never will; I just don't understand how that's even possible because crying would be in direct conflict with the actual emotion you're feeling—guess it's just over my head, then.

Straining against tears myself—only partly because I didn't want others to see me shedding tears, but mostly, honestly, because I didn't want them to get the wrong idea, to think I was crying for joy, because I was not——I walked off and smoked a cigarette. There was no joy in those tears. All I could think about for the next half hour is how **HYPOCRITICAL** everyone is————————everywhere I go, it's all the same and I'm used to being alone, so don't get the wrong idea because if they don't want me a part of their fucking club, well, too bad because it's said to be non-inclusive and I need it just as much as you do!

Turn the page →

Selfies from Hell

279

280

281

282

283

284

285

286

Turn the page ➤

Eat Shit

289

Mr. President

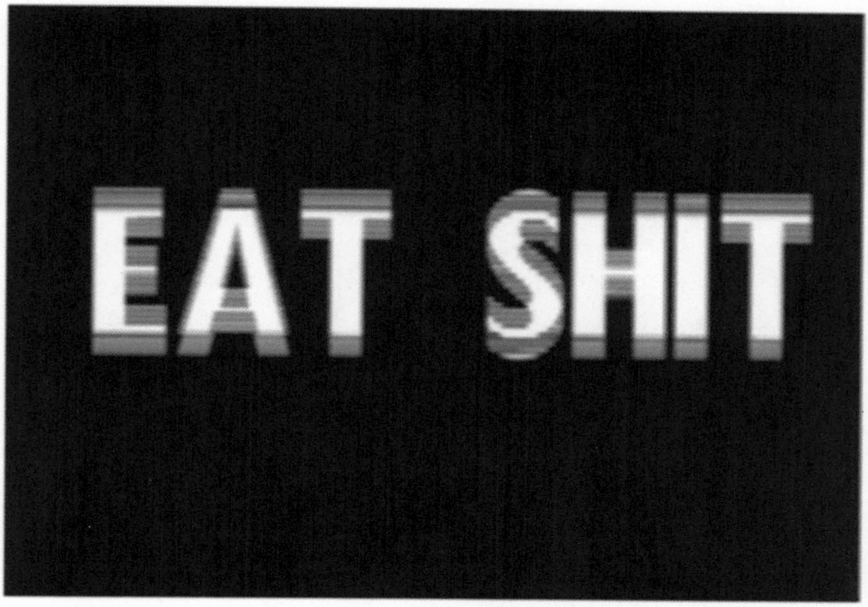
EAT SHIT

Mr. Police Man

293

Mr. Republican

295

Mr. Democrat

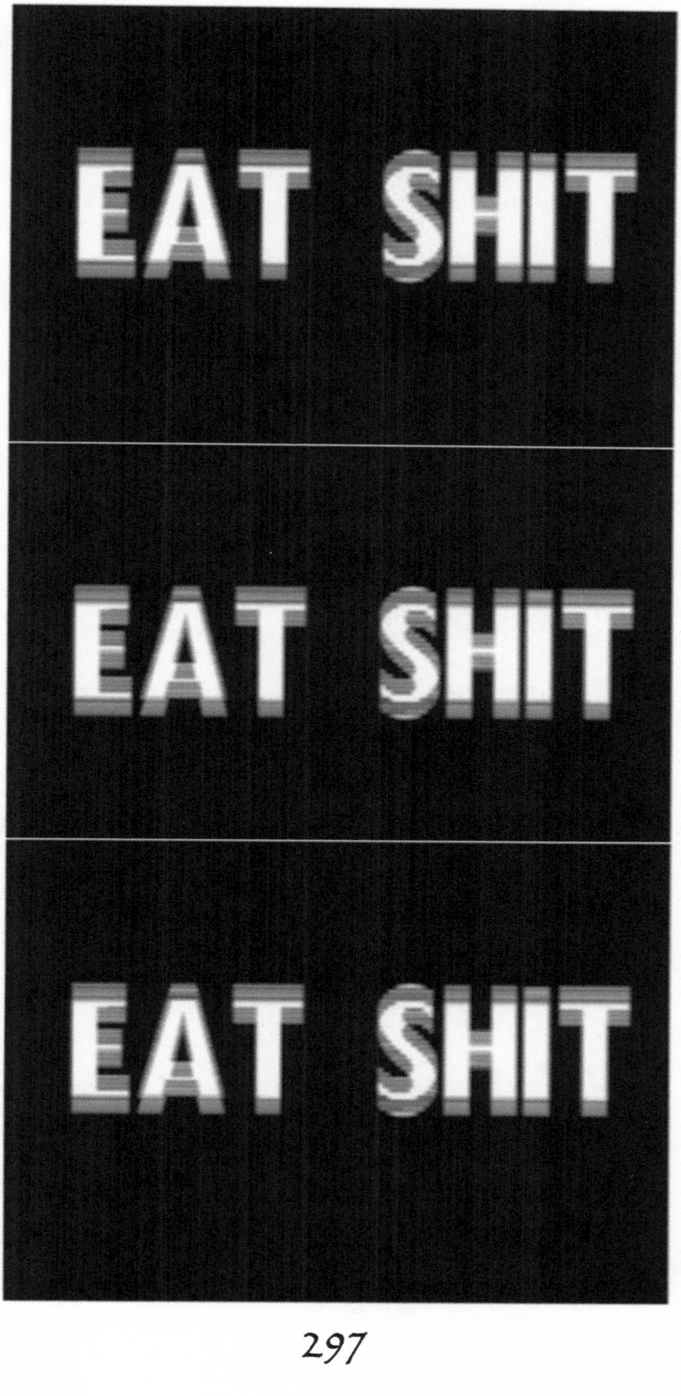
EAT SHIT
EAT SHIT
EAT SHIT

fuckin

motherfucker

Don't let the door hit you
on your way out. . .

and
If you like what you've seen here,
feel free to buy my other books.

www.chaoswriting.net

Credit Where Credit's Due

<u>You Made Me (Pp. 6)</u>: "If you're offended by this [song], good, because I'm offended by the way I had to grow up. So who's really been slighted?" is a line in the song "White Trash Anthem" by Blood for Blood, from *Outlaw Anthems*.

<u>Word Attack (Pp. 7)</u>: "Word Attack" is the name of a song by the Adolescents, from their self-titled album.

<u>Demolition Dancing (Pp. 9)</u>: "Demolition Dancing" is the name of a song by the Ruts, from their album entitled *The Crack/Grin And Bear It*.

<u>A Cunt Rawker (Pp. 17)</u>: "Cunt Rock" is the name of a song by Chaotic Dischord, from their album *Very Fuckin' Bad*.

<u>Thicker Than Blood (Pp. 23)</u>: I'm in the center. To my right is my friend Mike Castelline.

<u>FUNdamentalism (Pp. 61)</u>: "There's no fun in fundamentalism" is a song by NOFX, from their album *7 Inch of the Month Club*.

<u>The Drones (Pp. 86)</u>: The Drones are a British Punk band, from 1977-1993.

<u>Everything Turns Gray (Pp. 98)</u>: "Everything Turns Gray" is a song by Agent Orange, from their album *Living in Darkness*.

<u>A Rip Off (Pp. 114)</u>: "Phuck" is shaped similar to the Phish logo.

<u>Unrestricted Self-Expression (Pp. 121)</u> : "I disapprove of what you say, but I will defend to the death your right to say it" is a quote by Evelyn Beatrice Hall in her book about Voltaire.

<u>Love to Hate (Pp. 136)</u>: "I Love to Hate" is the name of a song by Screeching Weasel, from their album *Boogadaboogadaboogada*

<u>The Real Reality (Pp. 150)</u>: "The real reality" is a line in a song called "Reality" by Chron Gen, from their album *The Best of Chron Gen*.

Hero or Vagrant? (Pp. 151): Henry the Barbarian is my friend Thurston Smyrski.

Thicker Than Blood (4) (Pp. 161): I'm on the left. To my right is my friend Mike Fink. "Make Guns Not Love for America" is a song by No Alternative. "Hated and Proud" is an album by Iron Cross.

A Lookalike (Pp. 167): Sid Vicious was the bassist of the Sex Pistols. Darby Crash was the singer of the Germs. Stiv Bators was the singer of the Dead Boys.

I'm Angry (Pp. 171): "I'm angry, and I've got the right" is a line from the song "Angry" by the Forgotten Rebels, from their album *Tomorrow Belongs to Us*.

Hey Goth (Pp. 184): "Hey Goth" is the name of a song by Chaotic Dischord, in which they sing "Hey Goth fuck off," from their album *Very Fuckin' Bad*.

Tonight (Pp. 191): "Tonight we're gonna fuck shit up" is a line from the song "Fuk Shit Up" by the Blatz, from their album *Blatz/Filth Shit Split*.

Purity (Pp. 195): "Hatred is purity" is a line from the song "Foreign Policy" by Fear, from their album *The Record*.

<u>Paranoid Adolescence (Pp. 204)</u>: "It's not my imagination, there's a gun on my back" is the opening line in the song "Revenge" by Black Flag, from their album *Jealous Again*.

<u>The Business (Pp. 208)</u>: The Business is a British Punk band.

<u>Wrecking Crew (Pp. 215)</u>: "Wrecking Crew" is a song by the Meteors, from their album *Curse of the Mutants*.

<u>Like Screaming at a Wall (Pp. 229)</u>: "Screaming at a Wall" is a song by Minor Threat, the chorus of which goes "It's like screaming at a wall. Someday it's gonna fall." The song can be found on their self-titled EP.